MORE POEMS ABOUT MONEY

MORE POEMS ABOUT MONEY

DANIEL WOLFF

FOUR WAY BOOKS
TRIBECA

LIBRARY OF CONGRESS CATALOGING-IN-PUBLICATION DATA
Names: Wolff, Daniel J., author.
Title: More poems about money / Daniel Wolff.
Description: [New York] : Four Way Books, [2022]
Identifiers: LCCN 2022003859 | ISBN 9781954245280 (trade paperback) | ISBN
9781954245341 (epub)
Subjects: LCGFT: Poetry.
Classification: LCC PS3573.O5295 M67 2022 | DDC 811/.54--dc23
LC record available at https://lccn.loc.gov/2022003859

This book is manufactured in the United States of America and printed on
acid-free paper.
Four Way Books is a not-for-profit literary press. We are grateful for the assistance
we receive from individual donors, public arts agencies, and private foundations
including the NEA, NEA Cares, Literary Arts Emergency Fund, and the
New York State Council on the Arts, a state agency.

PROUD MEMBER

[clmp]

We are a proud member of the Community of Literary Magazines and Presses.

CONTENTS

Prologue

There can't be more poems about money
because there haven't been any.
Nothing deep or funny
about a penny.
It isn't even real.
What people lose sleep over, kill to collect,
hoard, squander, steal—
is a promise. Inspect
the coin more closely;
it has no value. Only stands
for value: gold we're mostly
told. What the teller hands
over—the un-poetic teller—
is a symbol. Legal. Tender.

BOOM

THE NEW TRIANGLE TRADE

I

Tonight, we see the eyes again.
And pretend they're the lights of the cars ahead,
red from stopping.
Tonight, we pretend nobody's watching
and that soon we'll leave them behind.

Tonight, in the brush by the side of the road,
kids creep out to the metal serpent,
puncture its million-dollar skin,
and suck their end of the hose.
We pretend we don't have to pay.

Tonight, we run on credit.
Tonight, we've taken a loan for speed:
the roar of our passage shackles their bodies,
carries them, stacked, to the edge of the ocean,
and packs them away in chains.

Tonight, we see the eyes again
and pretend we'll all survive the journey—
pretend we'll depart from a sun-beat coast
to land in a place that's green and new—
pretend we have nothing to trade.

2

To the south of what we call our nation,
the scattered ruins of sugar plantations
—like tiny islands or dying reefs,
like a set of slowly eroding beliefs—
are preserved to serve as tourist attractions.
What chained some set others free:
to sightsee, to study emancipation,
to sample exotic recipes:

> *Take rum derived from rape. Sweeten.*
> *Add tropical flavor. Shake until all sense is beaten*
> *out. Serve cold, impossibly*
> *cold.*

Our job is only to sip slowly
and disregard the impending death
of ice: by-product of our very breath.

3

The street that sleeps on merchandise
wakes to a sore back. Aches all day.
Finds it hard to find the smile
to paste above the fashion boots.

The street that spreads its legs for pay
can't shut down at night.
Its sign—FOR SALE!! EVERYTHING GOES!!—
points to the sky, the ground, the sea.

The street that was once industrial space—
that colonized the sweet and raw,

transforming the goods of island nations
by adding value, civilization—

now that street stripped-down reveals
that all it can sell is what it was:
guidebooks offer maps to trace
the graves of the famous dead.

And death itself, the street insists,
is out of fashion, an old arrangement.
That which was once the Triangle Trade
long since erased—or sold.

The street that sleeps on merchandise
wakes to bits of information
embedded like chips in brand new bodies
stacked and shipped in nylon chains.

MONEY IS PROPERTY

The sum of the vectors of a triangle delivers
the shiver
of the present: not new really, not even young,
but the only home we have among
brute calculations. If we've flung away our future
—indentured
our past for that better tomorrow—if we will
always owe the bank—still we must be thankful.
All our work is finally worth
the sum we place on a piece of earth.
Is that, or is that not,
a plot?

MONEY IS WAR

On the ground, a sound like a cat fight.
In the air, the howl of zigzag lines
scratching the undivided night.
Next door, the neighbor reclines
in peace. And so does the next. And next: each silhouette
on its own chair, with its own porch and asphalt
drive, its own access to the tired harbor, ill-met
for decades now. The assault
has been ceaseless: soldiers
digging bodies into sand, all to penetrate
imagined borders. Why? On whose orders?
All we wanted was some private
property: a strip on which to land.
Our want, their command.

PROFIT

Consigned to define profit,
we say: "Profit is winning. Profit is what gives play
meaning." Meaning the play

of the market: the way
we acquire and trade that which we're
consigned. To define profit

is to lose, is to stop.

THE POOR MAN'S WEALTH

"The certaine knot of peace . . . the poor man's wealth . . . "

—Sir Philip Sidney, "Come Sleep! O Sleep!"
Astrophel and Stella

Water cut. Gas cut. The dim reflection
of the city caught in the wood floor, dirty.
Humped under blankets, a collection
of kids—maybe thirty—
most of them sleeping. Or trying to sleep.

Beyond the brick horizon, war.
The stairs
have been closed-off, the front door
chained. The sign says BEWARE—
but beware of what? Sleep?

One of them jimmied a window,
then climbed up the dream of a rope
and called for the others to follow:
breaking and entering in hope
of sleep.

They are profitless. And gain—through lawlessness and stealth—
their squat, their keep, their sleep, their wealth.

We have a noun for having nothing.
It may be modified or made an object.
It represents the state of being

without. Of being poor. Of seeing
but not being seen. If the market is a grammar,
we have a noun for having nothing.

It lets us write the sentence.

QUARRY

Where the concrete counterweight once weighed the horizon
—once swung into action
and hoisting a chunk from the rock face,
made profit out of negative space—

now the opposite:
bindweed and Queen Anne's lace
overtake at their vegetative pace
the abandoned blocks of granite.

Water smooths giant boulders
where cutters once gouged the future.
Now their descendants swing at the end
of ropes that send

them, screaming, into chill pools of progress.
The new world pursues a new quarry: happiness.

GOLD STANDARD

It's not like the world, like, *runs*.
Like it's night,
and then the dark gets counted down till it's *done*.
That's what they say, right?
I mean, they make it seem like everything, you know,
has this kind of *order* to it.
And you're *stupid* or something if you can't follow.
Bullshit.
It's not like you see *this* and then *that*. Like there's a frame
around it. Like you feel one thing at a time
and ought to be able to *name*
each one. There's no downbeat. You can't say, "I'm
here now; I get it." If you could find the exact word—the gold
standard—then, bam! it would be *said*. Which is, like, *heard*. Or sold.

LUCY AND ROGER
(MONEY IN THE BANK)

In the culture we grew up in
—rich in ways that war supported:
purported links hidden, as if
we lived in peace, or had no wealth—
in that manufactured culture,

the fact that Lucille Ball, the clown,
went to school with Roger Tory
Peterson, the famous birder,
seemed to us arbitrary. And
so: funny. Money in the bank.

Lucy was the TV redhead,
always pretty and in a fix:
eyes big and lips puffed out, trying
to avoid the consequences
we knew she'd have to pay someday.

Peterson was non-descript. He
wrote a guide to birds that made them
easier to know: descriptions
drawn so clearly we could check them
off our life-list. He and she had

no connection, except . . . except
profit where it's least expected:

proof the world makes different sense, as
arbitrary as a line break
each eight beats, as manufactured.

We laughed, of course. That they could share
the same history back before they
became who we knew they had to
be. Coincidence? Maybe. Or
symmetry. We laughed. And counted.

What is money?
Money is what's left over:
the momentum after
you release the sling
on the triangle
of the slingshot.
And then what've you got?
Money is the ability
to forget.

BUST

INFLATION

"Today's rising housing prices:
. . . the biggest bubble in history."
And how nice it is
to live inside! Like angels
lifted o'er the fray, the angles
of our wings slightly
off perhaps, but we flap
and happily: the light and air
piped in. If heaven proves a sticky trap,
who are we to care?
Our home's a cloud, our food
delivered, what fluctuations
mar the mood
but shimmers that we ride: inflations.

CREDIT
(DESIRE)

"The market runs on credit . . . "
which romantics call yearning.
A flame. Or a sonnet.
The perpetual burning
of what-we-are to manufacture
what-we-want. We borrow
on a future
that stays, each day, tomorrow.
You follow? We all do. The fuel,
fanned by beauty, just enough
beyond our reach to teach how cruel
love can be. Except it isn't love.
Or poetry. Or fire.
It's desire. The market runs on desire.

DARK MARKETS

"Systemic risk . . . derivatives . . . dark markets."
These whispers on the far horizon
ripple through our solid credit.
It seems the very air we lean on
leaves. Along the bubble's
sewn seam, a sighing.
Is risk what we've been flying on? The trouble
is when truth starts lying,
all the rest is derivation.
What we thought to save is spent,
and now, the long inflation
failing, we eye the veil; it's rent.
The boom becomes the hiss of trust
escaping. And then the bust.

LOANS AND TRUST

"We're caught in a system that doesn't work,
and we can't afford to let it fail."
The words of a man on his way to work.
His job is inventing real estate deals. Which fail,
he says, more often than not. "The work
depends on loans—and trust. Loans and trust are known to fail.
But for me to even get up for work,
I've got to believe the next won't. Fail."
Then, as the connected cars of his train work
their way underground, he adds that his marriage is about to fail.
"Has, really. Already has. We're trying to make it work
for the kids. But that can only last so long. Every morning we fail."
He looks out through the blackened window. "It doesn't work,"
he says again, "and we can't afford to let it fail."

UNEMPLOYMENT RATE

GM CUTS 10,000 JOBS
(An adjustment, merely, of the market's knobs.)
UNEMPLOYMENT AT 8.3
"Nothing to see
here, folks. Keep moving." Down Route 59,
a big plywood sign
—YABOO FENCE—
and under it, a thick tense
man with nothing to do: his whole crew
laid-off. "I never knew
it could be like this. Numbers, I guess, don't lie."
Until they do. HOW BEST CALCULATE
CURRENT JOBLESS RATE?
Go by. Go buy.

RECESSION
(CUL-DE-SAC)

It's not that nothing's left.
Take a right up the cul-de-sac
and stop at the McMansion.

It's empty. Listen:
bees boring perfect holes in the back
of new-laid planks.

Listen: the granite steps are stone deaf.
We built too big, too late,
and now we have to deal.

Kneel. Give thanks.
This is our estate,
real.

THE FINANCIAL NEWS

GM COLLAPSES!

Details to follow. Except NEWSPAPERS DISAPPEAR!

Contemporary synapses

demand speed, ear-to-ear.

Down the road, a couple divorces;

POLAR ICE CAP MELTS!

"Did trapping beaver for beaver pelts

open the way for invading forces?"

Peace, we forget, is just more of the same.

RATIONAL VISION OF MARKET TO BLAME!

Yet those who believe the system random

tend to be absent when profits are taken.

TRUST FUNDS TURN UP EMPTY!

Which leaves a silence. Which fills with history.

ECONOMIC CYCLES

THE ANSWER? CONSUMER CONFIDENCE
The more we believe, the more we buy;
hope floats the marketplace.

Until it doesn't. A cycle as commonplace
as flood and drought. "Don't worry about
the answer, consumer. Confidence

is all you need." And that's an order.

ECONOMIC CYCLES II

"Market shaky? Print more money."
Let us! Let us make more lettuce!
Let us scatter seed. Let us till the sunny
soil till brimming harvest
brings . . . what? Another loan.
A Ford we can't afford.
A flat TV. Home.
Extend, we're told, the extension chord.
And when there's no more left to spend?
Confess,
consumer: it mustn't end.
Worthless,
we're still worth our weight in . . . what? Want. Shop
till you drop that tiny seed: there can be no final crop.

ECONOMIC CYCLES III

"The market needs to find its bottom."
Falling through ever darker layers,
losing light, shedding investors,
till the last least loan has been cast off, rotten,
headlong flaming from the ethereal sky,
all desires are reduced to one:
how overcome
this dire calamity?

By striking land (or ash).
The market hasn't technically crashed
—and can't bounce back, can't start up again,
can't float its bargain
bonds again—till it's found
bottom. Our paradise, lost: a hole in the ground.

DEPRESSION (A WORKING DEFINITION)

"We aren't underwater. Not yet.
But I can feel the tide rising.
And see our stuff slowly sliding
away. The rug is wet;
the dining room set is overdue.
You stare at me across the table
like I should do
something. I do what I'm able
to. But I can already tell tomorrow's work
won't ever be enough.
You say something about love;
I don't think you know how badly we've been hurt.
Here's our home. Here's the hole it's in.
And here's the line where the ocean begins."

AFTERMATH

AFTERMATH

In the aftermath, peace.
Like the ocean after a whale:
the slight crease
where a house went under, a business failed.
And here, clinging to man-shaped debris,
an angel winged with giant waves.
He (or she) was brave
(or wasn't)—now awaits recovery.
Meanwhile, a shark in a three-piece suit plays
with a ragged cut of meat. What's lost
is only lost to view. It could be raised—
it could all be raised—but at what cost?
And why would we
sign on again, when the beast is still at sea?

DREDGE
(RECOVERY)

The big dredge dips its head
and mucks in the underwater,
then bends the horizon, straining to lift,
and breaking the surface, weeps.

> *We fuck things up. It's what we do.*
> *And having done so, we fuck them again.*
> That bucket contains the stinking remains
> of a thousand previous fixes.

Hear how the scavenger cries with delight
as the neck of the crane thrusts at the sky.
Watch as it drops its toxic load
into the patient, shuddering barge.

> And how does the barge deliver its cargo?
> As garbage—to cover our other blunders.
> *Each brave generation has to dig out from under.*
> *All heaven is built on fill.*

TUG
(INTO THE MARKET)

The screw of a tug stirs the night,
thrums the chest like a heart in blood.

Does it fight? Yes.
Its iron mass displaces fear

if fear is a kind of tide.
Inside its cabin, a wakeful captain

compares the bright ideal of charts
with what he sees outside.

The diesel pushes goods to port
and, whether or not it turns a profit,

turns away: back into the market.
Hear the hollow chest.

PEACE
(A WORKING DEFINITION)

Is this, then, peace?
Enough cash to rent a place on earth
and eat?

Out on the street, it's dusk.
A family sits on a stoop,
the mother's laughter soft as light.

She's lived to see the myth collapse.
Now she watches her children play
under trees she never planted.

AN INVASIVE SPECIES

We are an invasive species,
brazen as part of our occupation,
craven without knowing why. See these
cleared lots, where the beach plum
has been plowed under? Someone
will enclose that light,
force the sand to stay outside,
make sure the air's conditioned.

Any space a potential site—
given poured concrete, given plywood beams.
And all we need to sustain our dreams
is a tie-in back to the main.

See the turtle
climb the beach,
her shell a kind of solar panel?
She lays her eggs just up from the harbor
so her young will be able to reach the water
and start all over, again.
Even when we interrupt,
blind, they bump foundations.

No one needs to teach these
tricks; no one winds these clocks.
As long as sun has heated rock,
we've been an invasive species.

PROFIT II

She got bored with steady
and broke it off. That same weekend ("Crazy!"),
she hooked up with another, and he
yanked her skyward, lips still puffy.

In theory, we can fight
back. In theory, our bodies aren't sold at market,
are greater than mere profit.
In theory, she might

break free. But not on the winter beach
where the wind clips foam from the tops of waves
like stock. Not in the constant screech
of sand on sand. No one's that brave.

Inside, at a greasy counter,
an old woman cuts in front of her,
orders the Dinner Special to-go,
then pays with a plastic card. No,

she's been taught to believe
in abundance: the promised reprieve
of sweat-stained sheets,
the up-and-down as revolution. "What *is* this meat?"

the old one asks, like she

might be served up next. The story's

the same in all the glossies:

      SOON THERE WILL BE

      NO MORE FISH IN THE SEA

THE DISMAL SCIENCE

After a century and a half
of chopping back beach grass
and leveling dunes,
the lifeguard leaves at five.

In her place, she posts a sign
written in a common tongue:
SWIM AT YOUR OWN RISK.
Everyone understands

- that the sun will set in the west
- that our money is counted in dollars
- that the sea is not a woman
- that each breath is a game of chance

That's why the swimmer who wades in the dark
knows there's no one to hear his cry.
That's why the forces that drag him down
have no color or name.

Maybe the ocean follows rules,
but it's a dismal science, barely known.
It takes two days till the body's found
in the shallows just off the casino.

MONEY IS WAR
(AGAIN)

Still the small dusk, the suburban joke:
a chuckle of motors,
the hum of TV, faint smoke
from next door. Others
may scent THE END COMING,
but thanks to the circular sprinkle of money,
the present still comes up green.
What we mean
is what we have: no more, no less.
A car, some bikes, a power mower,
a hedge clipper, the other mess—
hung from the wall in stenciled order.
And that faint smoke that whispers through?
Not battlefield, but barbeque.

AH, THE POOR

Like the oaks which hold their bronze
for a reason
(we assign the reason)

and then on a windless day
drop their leaves one by one
(for the reason that their time has come)

and litter the ground with wealth while
leaving the design intact
(if, in fact, it is design),

like that we say:
"Ah, the poor!
They'll be with us always."

SCAFFOLDS OF RE-BAR
(A NATURAL ECONOMY)

Scaffolds of re-bar veined with vent pipe
hidden by drywall escalate upward
across the street from K.

Woman plumber in the last Renovation,
organizer in the Fall-Out that followed,
since the Recovery a stay-at-home mom.

She set up a workplace to sketch the light
that poured in off the eastern sea
but was never convinced it counted as work.

Then the corner became WHOLE FOODS.
And they cleared the flophouse across the way.
Now, they're building a NEW MUSEUM.

K has watched the sky reduce,
the shadow climb her unstained wall.
She's heard the morning pound towards profit

and—plumber, mother, organizer—
has come to believe that everyone's good,
but that good gets blocked by hurt.

K finds hope in the way the body

heals itself—as if we shared
a natural economy.

After she's dropped her kid at school,
she crosses the street to picket the site
where Art is taking the place of Life.

As the men on stilts tape and spackle,
she waves her placard back and forth,
trying to make a path to the sky.

ALTERNATIVES

THE WEALTH OF NATIONS

"Of that place beyond the heavens, none of our earthly poets has yet sung . . ."

—Plato, *Phaedrus*

On that vast ocean, an island of hope:
that place we dream of beyond the heavens

where justice will, at last, be done—
where nothing is ever forgiven.

It feels like starting over again:
the scattered ruins of sugar plantations,

a ceiling fan that slowly spins
(but this one redistributing wealth).

"Free enterprise," the palm trees hum,
"leads to begging, palsy, slums.

Here, we've just one class: the humble."
While shadows mumble at the edge of verandas,

billboards bark on the boulevard;
they re-explain the revolution:

YESTERDAY, WE WORKED FOR OTHERS.
TODAY, WE WORK FOR OURSELVES

A song that's sung beyond the heavens:

"The wealth of nations is everyone's wealth."

PLANNED ECONOMY

As it was improvised then (the war),
so it's guerilla now (the peace).
Carburetors cannibalized by a man

who once made hand grenades from tomato cans.
Peace is a work in progress now,
as it was improvised then. The war

can't be abandoned.

CALL THIS VICTORY

Call this victory:
no more hunger, no more poverty.
As the lights of the city announce the future,
a fisherman hooks a silver
promise and flops it up on the rocks.
Traffic continues to chew.
And in the sky below Orion's belt,
an airplane slips the embargo. You
fought, you won;
now, the silver shudders once
and stares a place in the sky.
The old gods hunt the new sea.
Call this victory.

EXCHANGE RATE

The island that doesn't believe in money
prints two kinds: a visitor's currency
(made to inflate a flat economy)
and the one slapped down on the domino table
or folded to fit under Grandma's skirts.

The first is only available
to a ruling class (which isn't supposed to exist),
the second a symbol of shared commodities:
"The Coin of Revolution Is Work."

Maybe it is. Or maybe it is
a dream that's yet to come true.

On an island where everyone's worth the same
—where you mean to me what I mean to you—
why do we make two kinds of change?

INHERITANCE
(THE SOCRATIC METHOD)

"Those who've managed to make their fortunes
love their money like mothers love children.
While those who inherit," so Socrates said, "are mostly indifferent:
pretend not to care where the trust gets spent."

So how did Socrates eat?

The cost of a cab from here to the river
is a third of the average monthly wage.
The painter (whose age
is the revolution's) makes his paintings on old newspaper.

Can you live on tobacco and rum?

Someone wakes early and prowls the shore,
searching under the rocks for treasure:
plastic bottles, two-by-fours.
If this is the currency—the current measure—

how many kids can sleep on a floor?

Yes, Jesus-the-Giant looks over us all.
Yes, He-in-Fatigues stares down from the wall.
Yes, the old moon still speaks in Greek.
(The spirit is willing, but production is weak.)

And yes, we inherit the wealth of nations.

PLATO STEALS THE RICE AND BEANS

> "Do you really think, my dear Menon, that anyone, knowing the bad things
> to be bad, still desires them?"
>
> —Plato, *Menon*

Plato enters as dachshund.
Waddles along the crowded streets,
sniffs at stains and broken shoes
but never asks a question.

Others do. In the crowds and cracks
of unfixed buildings,
the homemade tops that children spin
keep wanting to know if the floors are flat.

And down in the murk of the polluted harbor,
bits of plastic puzzle herring.
Who fail to fool the wheeling terns.
Who carry their questions almost to heaven.

Beyond (but just) the city limits
—on a tree-lined street near a research center—
the old comandante confronts the dilemma:
"Should age lead us back to the mountains?"

Meanwhile, Plato—the bulging dachshund—
considers with beady and pampered eye

the portion of rice and beans a family
of five is supposed to survive on.

"Can virtue ever be taught to creatures?"
"No," barks Plato, "it's divine in nature."

THE REVOLUTION HAS STALLED

The revolution has stalled.

Designed to improve the lives of all,
the revolution has stalled.

Was it crushed by the force of foreign commerce,
by overseas workers and underpriced malls?
The revolution has stalled.

A new generation wakes to see
the shade of a bright container ship
disappear behind Spanish walls.
The revolution has stalled.

Mistakes have been made, miscalculations.
"We fought our fight with the highest intentions."
But the child still sleeps in a dirty shirt
and wakes to the rooster's call.
The revolution has stalled.

Bread is cheap. What's become expensive
are the plastic bags to carry it home.
The woman in the wheel chair will sell you a couple,
but if you walk to the river, its sisters and brothers
are snagged in the rocks where the sewage falls.
The revolution has stalled.

Its pants are too old and big.
Giant machines once cut its seams
to match the legs of the power station,
but a pig now roots in the parking lot,
and according to the rules of the Five-Year Plan,
all lovers must circle the same stone wall.
The revolution has stalled.

What is ambition? A diesel engine
mounted in a '54 Buick.
When it jerks to a stop at the foot of a hill,
you pop the hood—and hundreds gather:
they all want to know what's failed.
"Nothing has failed! Nothing is final.
Those who would run must first learn to crawl."
The revolution has stalled.

Across the harbor, in the Spanish castle,
the tortured are turned into soldiers and martyrs.
When something is broken, you save the parts:
the old stars jimmied into new constellations,
into Catholic thrones, into khaki saints.
If hope is a mix of tobacco and rum
(the present a product of the Triangle Trade),
how do you dance—how do I dance—how do we dance at the Cannibal's
    Ball?
The revolution has stalled.

EXCHANGE

NAKED WE LAND ON EARTH

Naked we land on earth.
Then strip its bounty
to cover our body.
We come to call that wealth.

The drill, the mill, the mine
are means to assume power.
Everything ends up ours
in time.

Every stranger
a potential lover.
Every question
an acquisition.

Call the current
currency—
 or sex—or property:
the need to get is constant.

When, naked, we leave the earth,
our net weight
is our net worth.
Strange how, when it's too late,

everything seems pre-ordained.
We pass through an exchange.

AS ALL THINGS CHANGE TO FIRE

As all things change to fire,
and fire exhausted
falls back into things,
the crops are sold
for money spent on food.

—Heraclitus, quoted in Plutarch's *On the E at Delphi*

As rows of red brick
piled up along the river
in three-story
raised structures
(brick fired
from river mud), couples abandoned
crops for city:
drawn by the promise—the spark—of money.

That's the first or ground story:
how the city
would lift them, how its brick
structures
(fueled by money)
would pull them skyward on a river
of . . . what? Of fire.
"All ye who enter here, abandon

hope." Their kids, city-
bred, discovered the real structure

of money:
that it flows, like a river,
to its own—and in time will abandon
all others. Here, then, the second story:
that the promise of brick
was a trap. And its only cure was fire.

Long abandoned,
left to rot by the stained river,
their generation set fire
not just to the city
but to their homes, their hopes, their money—
to the very idea of structure.
What was left was a story
written in ashes and blackened piles of brick.

It was the third generation—the city-
children's children—who abandoned
brick
altogether and followed the river
back out to the country—to a new structure,
a subdivision of money,
supposedly fear- and fire-
proof: a distant, different, safer story.

If the city
today still looks abandoned—
if you can still trace the story
of betrayal and fire
in stunted children and brick

rubble—see among the river-
front structures,
investors eyeing the return of money.

As bricks will shift inside a structure—
as a city abandons and embraces its river—as a story
sets and re-sets language—fire changes back into money.

DEEPWATER HORIZON

I

Ill-plumed, the sea crashes.
Men in wetsuits try to re-boot,
while their wives and daughters wait in factories,
hands gnarled over nothing.

An aerial shot reveals a hole in the earth.
What gushes darkly through blue water
isn't life-blood but power. Or the makings of power:
that which will someday be refined.

If we could gain control, then what?
Or more to the point, how long?
Sea turtles scrim sand beaches, dig shallow ovals,
but what they deposit will be covered in tar.

Far out on the curved horizon, a rig rides heroic.
We rule. From the frail call of the least tern
to the blue fluke of the giant tuna,
our hunger trumps.

Already it drapes the coral reef
in still ribbons of black.

2

We are the wick, love.
That probes the very core of earth

and draws its fuel along our length.
We can't help it; it's our nature.

Even if we're careful
—and cut the air before we go
—walk to where we shop
—buy what harms us least,

our every act consumes.
We leave a tiny trail of ash.
Multiply that by how many we are;
subtract the total from the silver bubble:

no wonder if the world we ride
flames out as it goes. We, love, are the fuse.

3

The well's been capped.
The wealth's been kept.
The wrong long done, we've closed the trap.
The barrels of black and yellow tears have all (for now) been wept.

We may curse what comes to pass
—our kids may learn to beg for water—
but once again the pools of gas
flow through forms, metered.

Inside our lives of light and cool,
the darkness we suppress

underlines our golden rule:

what we want is what works best.

The well's been capped; the wind blows free.

How blue the surface of the new-scrubbed sea.

ENVOI

It is all—and we are in—an exchange.
It transports us in man-made chains.
We may think we command the deck
but we won't—and can't—turn back.
It is all—and we are in—an exchange.

The need to trade is the need to touch.
The stuff that we desire so much
breaches in the sea between us:
booms and busts, booms and busts.
The need to trade is the need to touch.

If we were equals, there would be no market:
the difference is what makes the profit.
Though we can dream an alternative,
we barely forget, never mind forgive.
If we were equals, there would be no market.

Allow me to give you all my money.
Pretend we share a common currency.
Join me as I stop at the village square
and toss my savings in the morning air.
Allow me to give you all my money.

Allow me to give you all my money.
If we were equals, there would be no market.

The need to trade is the need to touch.

It is all—and we are in—an exchange.

APPENDIX

Such is my debt I may not say forgive,
But as I can, I'll pay it while I live;

> —Anne Bradstreet, "To Her Father with Some Verses," 1650

Wisdom is sold in the desolate market where none come to buy . . .
It is an easy thing to rejoice in the tents of prosperity . . .

> —William Blake, "The Four Zoas, Night the Second," 1797

Those who hold, and those who are without property, have ever formed
distinct interests in society.

> —James Madison, *The Federalist Papers*, No. 10, 1787

Words are the money of the ideological market of mankind.

> —Christopher Cauldwell, *Illusion and Reality*, 1937

But Rapture's Expense
Must not be incurred
With a tomorrow knocking
And the Rent unpaid –

> —Emily Dickinson, "Rather arid delight", undated

We will never see an end of ructions, we will never have a sane and steady
administration until we gain an absolutely clear conception of money.

> —Ezra Pound, *What Is Money For?*, 1939

. . . there is on Earth just so much Gold, so many Things, so many Men, so many Desires: As many of those Desires as any thing can satisfy, so much is it worth of another thing, so much Gold it is worth.

—Bernardo Davanzati, "A Discourse upon Coins," 1588

. . . money is a social rather than an economic phenomenon, a kind of myth or belief universally held in society.

—Pierre Vilar, *A History of Gold and Money, 1450–1920*, 1976

ACKNOWLEDGEMENTS

The first section of "Deepwater Horizon" appeared in slightly different form in *The Evergreen Review* and a modified version of the entire poem in *Counterpunch*. "Tug (Into the Market)" appeared in *TLM*.

ABOUT THE AUTHOR

Daniel Wolff, as poet, has published three previous collections and a chapbook, made appearances in many literary magazines, been anthologized, collaborated with dancers, sculptors, and print-makers, mailed fictitious letter-poems, done performance pieces, printed broadsides, tacked poems up illegally in subway cars and installed them in peep-shows. He's read across the country as well as on air. He's also published a number of award-winning books as non-poet.

PUBLICATION OF THIS BOOK WAS MADE POSSIBLE BY GRANTS AND DONATIONS. WE ARE ALSO GRATEFUL TO THOSE INDIVIDUALS WHO PARTICIPATED IN OUR 2021 BUILD A BOOK PROGRAM. THEY ARE:

Anonymous (16), Maggie Anderson, Susan Kay Anderson, Kristina Andersson, Kate Angus, Kathy Aponick, Sarah Audsley, Jean Ball, Sally Ball, Clayre Benzadón, Greg Blaine, Laurel Blossom, adam bohannon, Betsy Bonner, Lee Briccetti, Joan Bright, Jane Martha Brox, Susan Buttenwieser, Anthony Cappo, Carla and Steven Carlson, Paul and Brandy Carlson, Renee Carlson, Alice Christian, Karen Rhodes Clarke, Mari Coates, Jane Cooper, Ellen Cosgrove, Peter Coyote, Robin Davidson, Kwame Dawes, Michael Anna de Armas, Brian Komei Dempster, Renko and Stuart Dempster, Matthew DeNichilo, Rosalynde Vas Dias, Kent Dixon, Patrick Donnelly, Lynn Emanuel, Blas Falconer, Elliot Figman, Jennifer Franklin, Helen Fremont and Donna Thagard, Gabriel Fried, John Gallaher, Reginald Gibbons, Jason Gifford, Jean and Jay Glassman, Dorothy Tapper Goldman, Sarah Gorham and Jeffrey Skinner, Lauri Grossman, Julia Guez, Sarah Gund, Naomi Guttman and Jonathan Mead, Kimiko Hahn, Mary Stewart Hammond, Beth Harrison, Jeffrey Harrison, Melanie S. Hatter, Tom Healy and Fred Hochberg, K.T. Herr, Karen Hildebrand, Joel Hinman, Deming Holleran, Lillian Howan, Thomas and Autumn Howard, Catherine Hoyser, Elizabeth Jackson, Jessica Jacobs and Nickole Brown, Christopher Johanson, Jen Just, Maeve Kinkead, Alexandra Knox, Lindsay and John Landes, Suzanne Langlois, Laura Lauth, Sydney Lea, David Lee and Jamila Trindle, Rodney Terich Leonard, Jen Levitt, Howard Levy, Owen Lewis, Matthew Lippman, Jennifer Litt, Karen Llagas, Sara London and Dean Albarelli, Clarissa Long, James Longenbach, Cynthia Lowen, Ralph and Mary Ann Lowen, Ricardo Maldonado, Myra Malkin, Jacquelyn Malone, Carrie Mar, Kathleen McCoy, Ellen McCulloch-Lovell, Lupe Mendez, David Miller,

Josephine Miller, Nicki Moore, Guna Mundheim, Matthew Murphy and Maura Rockcastle, Michael and Nancy Murphy, Myra Natter, Jay Baron Nicorvo, Ashley Nissler, Kimberly Nunes, Rebecca and Daniel Okrent, Robert Oldshue and Nina Calabresi, Kathleen Ossip, Judith Pacht, Cathy McArthur Palermo, Marcia and Chris Pelletiere, Sam Perkins, Susan Peters and Morgan Driscoll, Patrick Phillips, Robert Pinsky, Megan Pinto, Connie Post, Kyle Potvin, Grace Prasad, Kevin Prufer, Alicia Jo Rabins, Anna Duke Reach, Victoria Redel, Martha Rhodes, Paula Rhodes, Louise Riemer, Sarah Santner, Amy Schiffman, Peter and Jill Schireson, Roni and Richard Schotter, James and Nancy Shalek, Soraya Shalforoosh, Peggy Shinner, Anita Soos, Donna Spruijt-Metz, Ann F. Stanford, Arlene Stang, Page Hill Starzinger, Marina Stuart, Yerra Sugarman, Marjorie and Lew Tesser, Eleanor Thomas, Tom Thompson and Miranda Field, James Tjoa, Ellen Bryant Voigt, Connie Voisine, Moira Walsh, Ellen Dore Watson, Calvin Wei, John Wender, Eleanor Wilner, Mary Wolf, and Pamela and Kelly Yenser.